SECOND SPACE

SECOND SPACE

New Poems

CZESLAW

MILOSZ

TRANSLATED BY THE AUTHOR
AND ROBERT HASS

An Imprint of HarperCollinsPublishers

*These translations were originally done by Robert Hass and Czeslaw Milosz,
except "Eyes," which was translated by Milosz and Renata Gorczynski.
Anthony Milosz supervised and corrected the editing of the final manuscript,
with assistance from Agniezska Kosinska.*

HarperCollins books may be purchased for educational, business, or sales
promotional use. For information, please write: Special Markets Department,
HarperCollins Publishers Inc., 10 East 53rd Street, New York, NY 10022.

FIRST EDITION

Designed by Mia Risberg

Library of Congress Cataloging-in-Publication Data

Milosz, Czeslaw.
[Poems. English. Selections]
Second space: new poems/Czeslaw Milosz.—1st ed.
p. cm.
Translated by Robert Hass.
ISBN 0-06-074566-5
1. Milosz, Czeslaw—Translations into English. I. Title.

PG7158.M553A24 2004
891.8'517—dc22 2004046949

04 05 06 07 08 BVG/RRD 10 9 8 7 6 5 4 3 2 1

Contents

PART II

PART III

PART IV

PART V

PART I

SECOND SPACE

How spacious the heavenly halls are!
Approach them on aerial stairs.
Above white clouds, there are the hanging gardens of paradise.

A soul tears itself from the body and soars.
It remembers that there is an up.
And there is a down.

Have we really lost faith in that other space?
Have they vanished forever, both Heaven and Hell?

Without unearthly meadows how to meet salvation?
And where will the damned find suitable quarters?

Let us weep, lament the enormity of the loss.
Let us smear our faces with coal, loosen our hair.

Let us implore that it be returned to us,
That second space.

LATE RIPENESS

Not soon, as late as the approach of my ninetieth year,
I felt a door opening in me and I entered
the clarity of early morning.

One after another my former lives were departing,
like ships, together with their sorrow.

And the countries, cities, gardens, the bays of seas
assigned to my brush came closer,
ready now to be described better than they were before.

I was not separated from people, grief and pity joined us.
We forget—I kept saying—that we are all children of the King.

For where we come from there is no division
into Yes and No, into is, was, and will be.

We were miserable, we used no more than a hundredth part
of the gift we received for our long journey.

Moments from yesterday and from centuries ago—
a sword blow, the painting of eyelashes before a mirror
of polished metal, a lethal musket shot, a caravel
staving its hull against a reef—they dwell in us,
waiting for a fulfillment.

I knew, always, that I would be a worker in the vineyard,
as are all men and women living at the same time,
whether they are aware of it or not.

IF THERE IS NO GOD

If there is no God,
Not everything is permitted to man.
He is still his brother's keeper
And he is not permitted to sadden his brother,
By saying that there is no God.

IN KRAKOW

On the border of this world and the beyond, in Krakow.
Tap-tap on the foot-worn flagstones of churches,
Generation after generation. Here I came to understand
Something of the habits of my brothers and sisters.
The nakedness of a woman meets the nakedness of a man
And completes itself with its second half
Carnal, or even divine,
Which is likely the same thing,
As revealed to us in the Song of Songs.
And must not every one of them nestle down into the Eternally
    Living,
Into His scent of apples, saffron, cloves, and incense,
Into Him who is and is coming
With the brightness of glowing wax candles?
And He, divisible, separate for each of them,
Receives them, him and her, in a wafer, into their own flame.
They shade the glow of it with their mossy-misty costumes,
They wear masks of silk, porcelain, brass, and silver,
So as not to mislead with their own, ordinary faces.
Little crosses on the marble will adorn their tombs.

FRAMING

"La Pologne est un pays marécageux où habitent les Juifs."*
(Poland is a marshy country where Jews live.)

Tragedy, Patrick, needs a proper framing
Of fractured rocks and abysmal chasms.
But I was describing a sandy plain,
Geese on a strip of grass, the grayness and indistinctness
Of a country hardly heard of,
For its sadness has no hands, no faces.

I had to write, Patrick. I was called,
Or compelled by pangs of conscience.
I tried as I could, in anger and impotence,
Without believing anybody in the world needed it.
You know how powerfully we are moved
By causes other than love of beauty. A style
Even gains by such deviations
From the rules of modernism under the force of passion.

Fickleness—I had a touch of it.
Also trinkets disguised my misery.
I could hardly stand peeling walls, dirt, garbage heaps.
Ugliness, which seems to invite misfortune.
But it was the given. And no water
Could wash away what was branded in our memories.
And something had to be done with it.
Something had to be done.

* Geography of Europe, according to the French (1939).

WERKI*

An English horn, a drum, a viola making music
In a house on a hill amidst forests in autumn.
A large view from there onto bends of the river.

I still want to correct this world,
Yet I think mostly of them, and they have all died.
Also about their unknown country.
Its geography, says Swedenborg, cannot be transferred to maps.
For there, as one has been, so one sees.
And it is possible even there to make mistakes; for instance,
        to wander about
Without realizing you are already on the other side.

As I, perhaps, just dream those rusty-golden forests,
The glitter of the river in which I swam in my youth,
The October from my poems with its air like wine.

The priests taught us about salvation and damnation.
Now I have not the slightest notion of these things.
I have felt on my shoulder the hand of my Guide,
Yet He didn't mention punishment, didn't promise a reward.

* Werki is a small area near Vilnius, Lithuania.

ADVANTAGE

It's not difficult to have them at a disadvantage,
Since they are no longer alive.
I sit with them at a table. It's summer, before the war.
The whole pension: I can do with them
Whatever I want, even make them memorable.
What a perverse game, from a sixteen-year-old kid
Arrogant out of misery and shyness,
Who just keeps silent and smiles stupidly—
Since a conversation about Schopenhauer was obviously not
For the likes of them. They suspect that he is not normal,
And in these matters they are usually competent,
Since they "know life"; i.e., the disreputable zone
Underneath all the polite prattle.
And now I have you in my power, you wretches.
One might say I am a chaplain of shadows.
Here, no more gossip, no more amorous touching
While you half-listen to my bitter talk.
What would you gain if I unveil my secret?
And what would I gain?
At stake was how one pays.
I often envied you. Nina, Ed.
Had you been able to guess bits of my destiny,
Perhaps you would bear your mediocrity with more ease.
With me here is the memory of a great illusion.
Not proud. I was lower than was your circle
Of mortal monads, servants of the flesh.
So what if I won't perish entirely,
If I leave an oeuvre, since the balance
Is uncertain. I don't know. Perhaps I was right,
Yet in truth, this wasn't what I wanted.

A MASTER OF MY CRAFT

In memory of Jaroslaw Iwaszkiewicz

In his poems was I seduced by the purity of color
Or by his love affair with death?
For without doubt he fell in love with death.
For him it was the truth and the entire content of the illusion
      of being.

It takes away
Towers of rosy gold,
The pale green marble of piazzas,
Violet-colored skies,
The red passage of a flute.

It silences forever a lover's groan:

In lilac-colored cinders,
Amidst stubble fields and grayness,
Like an orange stain,
The flaming bush of your nakedness.

I think now that there is something indecent in this Dionysiac
      sweetness of dying.
The passing away of people and things is not the only secret of time.
Which calls us to overcome the temptation of our serfdom.
And to put on the very edge of the abyss a table,
And on the table, a glass, a pitcher, and two apples,
So that they magnify the unattainable Now.

A STAY

My stay in that city was like a dream
And the dream lasted for years.

I was, in fact, not interested in anything
So long as I heard a voice dictating verses.

And in that way I invented a life,
And thus my destiny was being fulfilled.

Some people believed that I was theirs,
So they put trust in my disguises.

I reproach myself for that,
For I wanted to be different,
Trustworthy, brave, noble-minded.

Later on I would only say: why reach so high?
I am and will be lame,
Which is no one's concern.

ON OLD WOMEN

Invisible, dressed in clothes too big for me,
I take a walk, pretending I am a detached mind.

What country is this? Funereal wreaths, devalued medals,
a general avoidance of remembering what happened.

I think of you, old women, silently fingering past days
of your lives like the beads of your rosaries.

It had to be suffered, endured, managed.
One had to wait and not wait, one had to.

I send my prayers for you to the Highest, helped
by your faces in old photographs.

May the day of your death not be a day of hopelessness,
but of trust in the light that shines through earthly forms.

CLASSMATE

I was walking toward her, carrying a half-opened rose.
I was riding, because it was a long journey.

Through a labyrinth of escalators, from a pit to a pit,
In the company of several phantasmagoric ladies.

She was stretched on a carpet, receiving guests,
Her neck a lily of immaculate whiteness.

Please kneel here, she said, next to me,
We are going to talk about the good and the beautiful.

She was gifted, produced graphomaniac poems.
This happened in another country, in a lost century.

She used to a wear a student cap adorned with wolf's teeth,
An emblem of our alma mater sewn into the velvet.

No doubt she married, had three children.
Who can track down these details?

Does the dream mean I desired her?
Or just felt pity for her former body?

So that it falls to me to count her scattered bones
Since I am the last from among that gang of youths from a century
        past?

A descent into a Dantesque dark hollow
Somewhere near Archangel or in Kazakhstan?

She should have been buried in the cemetery at Rossa,
But an evil fate no doubt carried her out of town.

Why her precisely, I don't understand.
I'm not sure I'd recognize her on a busy street.

And I ask myself why it is constructed so perversely:
So that life is vague and only death is real.

Farewell Piorewiczowna, unasked-for shadow.
I don't even remember your first name.

TENANT

It happened in Wilno, sometime after June 1940, when the city was overrun by the army of our Eastern neighbor.

An elderly lady, in financial straits since the state which paid her pension had ceased to exist, sublet a room to an officer of the rank, it seems, of captain.

He was a huge Russian, very polite, but completely taciturn.

He caused her no trouble, since he received no guests, neither men nor women; he left for work in the morning and returned in the evening.

Then he would either turn on his light to read or lie on his bed in the dark.

No one knew of what, exactly, his work consisted; perhaps it was of a kind calling for discretion.

His name will remain forever unknown to us, and we will never find out what was on his mind.

We can only guess that he was struggling with a completely new experience, i.e., an encounter with a civilization completely different from the one in which he grew up.

He had been taught that there was no God or devil, and so he marveled at the sight of crowds praying in churches.

It gave rise to a bitter feeling at the futility of human belief and of the supplications sent up to the throne of Absence.

It is probable that he meditated on evil, i.e., on the suffering inflicted on human beings by human beings.

And on the evil for which we, therefore, share responsibility, and on the question of what our obligations are in a world thus ordered.

If to say "no" to a command was indeed to curse the day of one's birth.

He shot himself one night, and the NKVD sealed his personal effects, his pistol and his books.

It would be indecent to say that he was greeted by angelic choirs, even though we have read in the Gospel, "Blessed are those who thirst for justice."

Most appropriate perhaps to keep silent about religion, for he disappeared without a trace among the millennia of the planet Earth, together with the uncountable others who have never ascended to any consolation.

GUARDIAN ANGEL

In my dreams my guardian angel takes the form of a woman,
Not always the same one. He knows that I, a fleshly creature,
Need a lover's touch. We don't make love,
But there is closeness between us, and understanding.

I never believed in the presence of angels, but my dreams have
    changed,
And when, recently, I found an underground grotto filled with
    treasure,
And we were moving the sacks together, I asked him
For one more moment of the dream, which gave me peace.

A BEAUTIFUL STRANGER

At a mirror, naked, pleasing to herself.
You really were pretty; let that moment last.
The rose-brown shields of your breasts,
A belly with a black tuft just recently grown.
And they would dress you immediately in languishing
Blouses, slips, wispy robes with trains.
You wore a corset in a fashionable shade of lilac,
On your thighs garters like the straps on armor.
They hung on you layers of ridiculous fabrics
So that you could take part in their theater
Of pretended ecstasies, smutty allusions.
A slave, and such you remain in the photograph
Dimmed by emulsion and the coloring of time.
Did you rebel? Yes, it is quite possible.
To know for yourself, not to tell anybody
And from the nothingness of their words,
To protect the wisdom of your mocking body.

And I, am I now liberated
From those rituals, masks, the floodlights of the ball?
Have I escaped the law that draws me
Into frozen fashions, half-dead manners?

I would like to save you, beautiful stranger.
Together we depart for eternal meadows.
You are naked again, and fifteen years old.
I take you by the hand, your promised one.
Think that nothing will happen to you
That was supposed to happen,
That you can be different,
That you are your own,
And not arrested by the exactness of a fate.

TO SPITE NATURE

Many misfortunes resulted from my belief in God,

Which was a part of my notion of the splendor of man.

Man, not withstanding his animal nature,
should have had a spiritual life of great richness,

Should have been directed in his behavior
by motives considered noble and sublime.

He earned respect by becoming a near-angel.

This is the image I found in the pages of romantic literature,

Backed by the biographies of martyred saints.

And I? Would I be any less? Should I regard myself as a less perfect
    being?

Alas, I found in myself only the instincts of a dominant male, of an
energetic spermatozoon.

What I wanted in truth was strength and fame, and women.

So I began to construct in myself feelings of love and of sacrifice.

Here a little tale about Meg and Johnny would be of use.

Johnny wanted Meg, for she lived in a palace
hardly accessible to him, a poor ragamuffin.

Or because she seemed a superterrestrial beauty,
too high for a low creature like himself.

Meg wanted Johnny because he seemed brighter than her other
    suitors

And because she knew her defects and was flattered at being his
    choice.

So a marriage occurred, and love, which was in fact two lonelinesses,
brought to both of them much torture, until they divorced.

This could have happened, or not.

In any case, I discovered that what fits me is a skeptical philosophy.

That doesn't ascribe to man any higher qualities,

Nor to the God man created.

Then I could be in harmony with my nature.

Yet I repeat "I believe in God," and I know
that my belief has no justification.

I SHOULD NOW

I should now be wiser than I was.
Yet I don't know whether I am wiser.

Memory composes a story of shames and amazements.

The shames I closed inside myself, but the amazements,
at a sun-streak on a wall, at the trill of an oriole, a face,
an iris, a volume of poems, a person, endure and return in
     brightness.

Such moments lifted me above my lameness.

You, with whom I fell in love, approach, and forgive me
my trespasses because I was dazzled by your beauty.

You were not perfect, but just that arch of eyebrow,
that tilt of the head, that voice, reticent and seductive,
could only belong to a perfect creature.

I swore to love you eternally, but later on
my resolution wavered.

My fabric is woven of flickering glimpses,
it wouldn't have been large enough to wrap a monument.

I was left with many unwritten odes in honor
of men and women.

Their incomparable bravery, devotion,
self-sacrifice passed away with them, and nobody knows of it.
Nobody knows for all eternity.

When I think of this, I need an immortal Witness
so that he alone knows and remembers.

HIGH TERRACES

Terraces high above the brightness of the sea.
We were the first in the hotel to go down to breakfast.
Far off, on the horizon, huge ships maneuvered.

In King Sigismund Augustus High School
We used to begin each day with a song about dawn.

I wake to light that warms
My eye
And feel Almighty God
Nearby.

All my life I tried to answer the question, where does evil come
        from?
Impossible that people should suffer so much, if God is in Heaven
And nearby.

NONADAPTATION

I was not made to live anywhere except in Paradise.

Such, simply, was my genetic inadaptation.

Here on earth every prick of a rose-thorn changed into a wound.
whenever the sun hid behind a cloud, I grieved.

I pretended to work like others from morning to evening,
but I was absent, dedicated to invisible countries.

For solace I escaped to city parks, there to observe
and faithfully describe flowers and trees, but they changed,
under my hand, into the gardens of Paradise.

I have not loved a woman with my five senses.
I only wanted from her my sister, from before the banishment.

And I respected religion, for on this earth of pain
it was a funereal and a propitiatory song.

HEAR ME

Hear me, Lord, for I am a sinner, which means I have nothing except prayer.

Protect me from the day of dryness and impotence.

When neither a swallow's flight nor peonies, daffodils and irises in the flower market are a sign of Your glory.

When I will be surrounded by scoffers and unable, against their arguments, to remember any miracle of Yours.

When I will seem to myself an impostor and swindler because I take part in religious rites.

When I will accuse You of establishing the universal law of death.

When I am ready at last to bow down to nothingness and call life on earth a devil's vaudeville.

SCIENTISTS

The beauty of nature is suspect.
Oh yes, the splendor of flowers.
Science is concerned to deprive us of illusions.
Though why it is eager to do so is unclear.
The battles among genes, traits that secure success, gains and losses.
My God, what language these people speak
In their white coats. Charles Darwin
At least had pangs of conscience
Making public a theory that was, as he said, devilish.
And they? It was, after all, their idea:
To segregate rats in separate cages.
To segregate humans, write off as a genetic loss
Some of their own species and poison them.
"The pride of the peacock is the glory of God,"
Wrote William Blake. There was a time
When disinterested beauty by its sheer superabundance
Gratified our eyes. What have they left us?
Only the accountancy of a capitalist enterprise.

MERCHANTS

In a town where a miracle occurred, merchants install their booths, side by side, along a street through which pilgrims proceed.

They display their goods, wondering at the stupidity which compels people to buy little crosses, tiny medals, rosaries.

Even plastic bottles in the shape of the Madonna for preservation of the healing water.

The sick on their stretchers, the paralyzed in their wheelchairs.

Fortify the merchants in their disdainful belief that religion is self-consolation, based on the understandable need for any kind of rescue.

They rub their hands, reckon, add to their inventory new supplies of crucifixes, or nickel coins imprinted with the effigies of popes.

And the pilgrims, looking at their faces, onto which have crept scarcely noticeable smiles, feel threatened in their faith, just as children feel threatened by grown-ups, keepers of a secret, guessed at, but still vague.

COFFER

Perhaps the world was created by the Good Lord to reflect itself in the infinite number of eyes of living creatures, or, what is more probable, in the infinite number of human consciousnesses.

Also of human fantasies, such as my romantic imagination of the forest in Raudonka or my imagination of the breasts of Miss Paula when I was in love with her.

Where does the Good Lord hide these images? Does He have a very large coffer in which He preserves all His treasures?

Or perhaps He is a grand computer in which unlimited numbers of them would find rest.

Maybe He's busy going through them, comparing the reflected images with what really happened.

Laughing into His beard at the wise men who maintained that there are only reflections and nothing else.

I

So strange, the self-loving "I" of men and women that adores itself in mirrors.

How many creams, rouges, ointments, starches for shirts, so that it appears exquisite to itself and glistens.

Yet just behind this facade the busy, invisible beauticians of Time are applying shadowy wrinkles to the angle of the eyes, drawing the lips into an expression of bitterness.

They pour ash on the hair, they change what had been unique into a nameless mask.

The mirror fades, the eyes hardly see. How difficult it is to believe that for the angels we are a singular event and not a number submitted to a universal law.

⌒

There is not the slightest doubt that that couple in Paradise were a one-time event.

Just think! Not to be committed to any law of dissolution!

Nor to the law of cause and effect.

Neither to the law of disagreement between the flesh and the will.

There was no "I." Only wonder.

The earth just lifted out of chaos.

Grass intensely green, riverbank mysterious.

And a sky in which the sun means love.

DEGRADATION

High notions of oneself are annihilated
by a glance in the mirror,
by the impotence of old age,
breath held in the hope that some pain
won't return.

Endless multitudes of people are humiliated thus,
as well as other mortal creatures
who seem to bear it with greater humility of spirit:
a falcon no longer fast enough to catch a pigeon,
a lame stork expelled by the sentence of his flock, which rises and
    flies away.
The wheel of the seasons, descending into earth.

What have the heavenly powers to say of this?
They take afternoon walks, they notice.
Here are we, and over there the so-called kingdom of Nature.
What's worse, consciousness or lack of consciousness?
Well, there weren't any mirrors in Eden.

NEW AGE

My body doesn't want to take my orders.
On a straight path it stumbles,
It has a hard time getting up stairs.
My attitude toward it is satirical. I laugh
At the flaccidity of my muscles, my dragging feet, my blindness,
All the parameters of deep old age.

Fortunately I continue to compose verses at night.
Though for what, when what I write down in the morning
I cannot make out later in the day.
I am helped by the enlarged font of a computer
Which I have managed to live long enough to see,
And which is an advantage.

EYES

My most honorable eyes, you are not in the best of shape.
I receive from you an image less than sharp,
And if a color, then it's dimmed.
And you were a pack of royal greyhounds once,
With whom I would set out in the early mornings.
My wondrously quick eyes, you saw many things,
Lands and cities, islands and oceans.
Together we greeted immense sunrises
When the fresh air set us running on trails
Where the dew had just begun to dry.
Now what you have seen is hidden inside me
And changed into memories or dreams.
I am slowly moving away from the fairgrounds of the world
And I notice in myself a distaste
For the monkeyish dress, the screams and drumbeats.
What a relief. To be alone with my meditation
On the basic similarity in humans
And their tiny grain of dissimilarity.
Without eyes, my gaze is fixed on one bright point,
That grows large and takes me in.

NOTEBOOK

To express. Nothing can be expressed.
Fire under a stove lid. Anastasia is making pancakes.
December. Before dawn. In a village near Jaszuny.

⌒

I should be dead already, but there is work to do.

⌒

From human speech to the muteness of verse, how far!

⌒

It spreads out, the valley, signs, lights.

⌒

The mild valley of those who are eternally alive.
They walk by green waters.
With red ink they draw on my breast
A heart and the signs of a kindly welcome.

⌒

To praise. Only this has been left
To the one who ponders, slowly,
Misfortune upon misfortune and from which side they struck.

⌒

People near me don't know how difficult it is to pretend that
    nothing happened, that everything is normal.

⌒

I loved God with all my strength on the sandy roads that wound
    through forests.

⌒

Where is the memory of those days that were your days on earth
And effectuated joy and pain and were for you the universe.

⌒‿

Low, beneath, in darkness,
A table and on it a thick book
And a hand inscribing something . . .

⌒‿

At the gate of Hell she stood, naked.

⌒‿

I want to describe the world as Lucretius did.
Yet there have been too many complications of late.
And the words in the dictionary are too few.
So I just say of the world, like Galileo: and yet it moves.

⌒‿

She slipped out of her panties, Lady Polixena.

⌒‿

My love in the dream, a squirrel in a hazel bush.

⌒‿

Cities! You have never been described.

⌒‿

The grown-ups led the cortege, deep in their stupid conversations.

⌒‿

The river Wilia flows, indifferent.

⌒‿

Stricken with pity and loathing.

MANY-TIERED MAN

When the sun rises
it illuminates stupidity and guilt
which are hidden in the nooks of memory
and invisible at noon.

Here walks a many-tiered man.
On his upper floors a morning crispness
and underneath, dark chambers
which are frightening to enter.

He asks forgiveness
from the spirits of the absent ones
who twitter far below
at the tables of buried cafés.

What does that man do?
He is frightened of a verdict,
now, for instance,
or after his death.

PART II

FATHER SEVERINUS

1. JACKDAWS ON THE TOWER

Jackdaws are perched on the tower outside my window.
Another year gone and nothing has come of my resolutions.
The cities, more and more populous, in an opulent sunset.
Awaiting the end, as then, in Antioch, Rome, and Alexandria.
A promise was given us, though it was two thousand years ago.
And you did not return, O Savior and Teacher.
They marked me with your sign and sent me out to serve.
I put on the burden of ecclesiastical robes
And the mask of a benevolent smile.
People come to me and force me to touch their wounds,
Their fear of death, and the misery of passing time.
Could I dare to confess to them that I am a priest without faith,
That I pray every day for the grace of understanding,
Though there is in me only a hope of hope?
There are days when people seem to me a festival
Of marionettes dancing at the edge of nothingness.
And the torture inflicted on the Son of Man on the cross
Occurred so that the world could show its indifference.

2. THEOPHILUS

The incurable illness of Theophilus.
Too zealous in his piety.
In his prayers God's mercy,
His care and love, renews itself.
I, watching the cruelty of his fate
Or perhaps of a preordained destiny,
Suffer. And I am deliberately hypocritical,
For I want to save him from loss of faith,
To save all people like him. Out of pity for them

Let us sing psalms, play music to Jehovah.
From our hearts let the walls of a powerful fortress
Rise around their believing hearts.
I cannot grasp why, and whence comes
My identity with them, perhaps divine?

3. KATIE

I do not understand why it should have been so,
That the Son of God had to die on the cross.
Nobody has answered that question.
How can I explain it to Katie?
She had read somewhere that the Majesty of the Creator
Had suffered offense which called for payment in blood.
Yes? So that He could, in a golden robe and a crown,
Observe from behind a cloud the scene of torture?
I say to her: a Mystery of Redemption.
And Katie? She does not want to be saved
At the price of the suffering of an innocent man.
Her father kneels every Sunday in his church,
Because what would you introduce in place of religion?
Perhaps the idiotic rituals of the Party,
Or football games ending in a brawl?

Pallas Athena was our goddess.
We sent delegates to the oracle at Delphi.
We walked in procession for Diana at Ephesus.
As it should be. The philosophers
Have not taken from the gods the glory due them.

I raise above the altar bread and wine.
Humbled, since my reason does not comprehend what I do.

4. HOW COULD YOU

It's beyond my understanding.
How could you create such a world,
Alien to the human heart, pitiless,
In which monsters copulate, and death
Is the numb guardian of time.

I am unable to believe that You wanted it.
There must have been some precosmic catastrophe,
A victory of the forces of inertia, stronger than Your Will.

A wandering rabbi who called You his Father,
A man defenseless against the laws and the beasts of this earth,
Disgraced, despairing,
Let him help me
In my prayers to You.

5. CARAVELS

To proclaim a man who bleeds from his wounds
A God and the ruler of the universe,
One must be crazy—a sufficient proof
That our species tends to reach for the impossible.

To place such a man at the center of the cosmos!
And to send out caravels armed with sails and the sign of the cross
To take possession of lands and seas.
To tidy up interstellar ships
And send them into the ocean of space and time.
Yet the man from the town of Nazareth
Who initiated all this was not a spirit.
His body, stretched on the tree of shame,
Suffered real torture, about which we try every day to forget.

6. PRESENCE

Lord, Your presence is so real that it weighs more than
    any argument.

On my neck and my shoulders I feel Your warm breath.

I pronounce the words of Your book, which are human,
Just as your love and hate are human.
You yourself created us in your image and semblance.

I want to forget the subtle palaces created by theologians.
You do not deal in metaphysics.

Save me from the images of pain I have gathered wandering
    on the earth,
Lead me where only Your light abides.

7. A CHILD

My robe, of a priest and a confessor,
Serves to cover up my uncertainty and fear.
We are disconnected people.
I envied the crowd's sureness in the world.

I felt I was a child instructing the grown-ups,
Giving advice like paper dams on a violent stream.

They needed me only in misfortune,
To conjure heavenly powers.
So they could come and be saved
From a tumor in the lungs or a viral infection.

There is a legion of us, intermediaries between what is high
And what is low.
We sprinkle water, we bless, we mumble.
They rebel against us again and again
Because they would like to converse with the boss himself,
Without intermediaries.
Yet are we not His voice that is like the voice of a man?

8. LEONIA

Can I tell them: there is no Hell,
When they learn on earth what Hell is?

In the confessional I listen to Leonia.
She fears damnation, which she thinks would be just.
If you don't get your due in this lifetime,
She says, you get it in the next.

There goes Leonia. Flames erupting
From sulfur lakes behind the gates of Hell.

9. AND IF

And if all this is only a dream
Mankind has about itself?
And we Christians
Are dreaming our dream within a dream?

And if nobody is responsible for this self-deception,
With which we go down into the earth
Expecting to be raised by Eternal Justice?

10. DREAD

To tell the truth, they believe and disbelieve.
They go to church lest someone think they are godless.
During the sermon they think of Julia's tits, of an elephant,
Of the price of butter, and of New Guinea.

He dared to think they might be like that
That night when He knelt in the Garden of Olives
And felt on His back the cold sweat of dread.

II. THE EMPEROR CONSTANTINE

I could have lived in the time of Constantine.
Three hundred years after the death of the Savior,
Of whom no more was known than that he had risen
Like a sunny Mithra among Roman legionnaires.
I would have witnessed the quarrel between *homoousios*
    and *homoiousios*
About whether the Christ nature is divine or only resembles divinity.
Probably I would have cast my vote against Trinitarians,
For who could ever guess the Creator's nature?
Constantine, Emperor of the World, coxcomb and murderer,
Tipped the scale at the Council of Nicea,
So that we, generation after generation, meditate on the Holy
    Trinity,
Mystery of mysteries, without which
The blood of man would have been alien to the blood of the universe
And the spilling of His own blood by a suffering God, who offered
    Himself
As a sacrifice even as He was creating the world, would have been
    in vain.
Thus Constantine was merely an undeserving tool,
Unaware of what he was doing for people of distant times?

And us, do we know what we are destined for?

PART III

TREATISE ON THEOLOGY

1. A YOUNG MAN

A young man couldn't write a treatise like this,
Though I don't think it is dictated by fear of death.
It is, simply, after many attempts, a thanksgiving.
Also, perhaps, a farewell to the decadence
Into which the language of poetry in my age has fallen.

Why theology? Because the first must be first.

And first is a notion of truth. It is poetry, precisely,
With its behavior of a bird thrashing against the transparency
Of a windowpane that testifies to the fact
That we don't know how to live in a phantasmagoria.

Let reality return to our speech.
That is, meaning. Impossible without an absolute point of reference.

2. A POET WHO WAS BAPTIZED

A poet who was baptized
in the country church of a Catholic parish
encountered difficulties
with his fellow believers.

He tried to guess what was going on in their heads.
He suspected an inveterate lesion of humiliation
which had issued in this compensatory tribal rite.
And yet each one of them carried his or her own fate.

The opposition, I versus they, seemed immoral.

It meant I considered myself better than they were.

It was easier to repeat the prayers in English
at the Church of St. Mary Magdalene in Berkeley.

Once, driving on the freeway and coming to a fork
where one lane leads to San Francisco, one to Sacramento,

He thought that one day he would need to write a theological
    treatise
to redeem himself from the sin of pride.

3. I AM NOT

I am not, and I do not want to be, a possessor of the truth.

Wandering on the outskirts of heresy is about right for me.

In order to avoid what people call "the serenity of faith,"
which is, after all, merely self-satisfaction.

My Polish compatriots have always liked the language of ritual
and disliked theology.

Perhaps I was like a monk in a mid-forest monastery
who, seeing from his window a river in flood,
wrote a treatise in Latin, a language entirely incomprehensible
to peasants in their sheepskin coats.

How ridiculous to deliberate on the aesthetics of Baudelaire
amidst the crooked fences of a little town
where hens rummage in the middle of a dusty street.

I used to turn for help to the Virgin Mary,
but I had difficulty recognizing her
in the deity elevated into the gilded fretwork of altars.

4. I APOLOGIZE

I apologize, most reverend theologians, for a tone not befitting the purple of your robes.

I thrash in the bed of my style, searching for a comfortable position, not too sanctimonious and not too mundane.

There must be a middle place between abstraction and childishness where one can talk seriously about serious things.

Catholic dogma is a few inches too high; we stand on our toes and for a moment it seems to us that we see.

Yet the mystery of the Holy Trinity, the mystery of Original Sin, the mystery of the Redemption are well armored against reason.

Which tries in vain to get straight the story of God before His creation of the world, and when the separation into good and evil occurred in His Kingdom.

What in all that can be grasped by little girls dressed in white for First Communion!

If even gray-haired theologians concede that it is too much for them, close the book, and invoke the inadequacy of the human tongue.

But it will not do to prattle on about soft little Jesus in the hay of His manger.

5. A BURDEN

Mickiewicz—why dabble with him if he has been sufficiently accommodated to everyday use?

Changed into a can of preserves which shows, when opened, a flickering film about an antique Poland.

And Roman Catholicism, is it not better to leave it alone?

So that the custom of sprinkling holy water is preserved, and the observation of holidays, and carrying the dead to carefully tended cemeteries.

Of course, there are people who would treat it seriously, i.e., politically.

I have never associated myself with those enemies of the Enlightenment who hear the devil speaking in the language of liberalism and in tolerance for all dissenters.

Alas, an American saying has applied to me, though it was not coined with kindly intent: "Once a Catholic, always a Catholic."

6. IN VAIN

Either gods are omnipotent and, judging by the world they
created, not good; or they are good, and the world slipped from
their hands, and so they are not omnipotent.

— THE SCHOOL OF EPICURUS

Six years old. I felt horror at the stony order of the world.

Later on, in vain, I sought shelter in colorful pictures of birds when I was the round-faced secretary of the Circle of Nature Lovers.

Charles Darwin, a clergyman-to-be, announced with regret his theory of natural selection, for he saw that it served the devil's theology

By proclaiming the triumph of the strong and the defeat of the weak, which is and has always been the devil's program, which is why he is called the Prince of This World.

Everything that creeps, runs, flies, and dies is an argument against the divinity of man.

I turned to anti-nature, i.e., to art, in order to build our home, along with others, out of the sounds of music and paint on canvas and the rhythms of speech.

Threatened at every moment, we marked our days on a calendar of stone or of paper.

Ready to be caught by a cold hand reaching out of the abyss to pull us down together with our unfinished task.

Yet we believed that some of us had received a gift, a grace, to spite the force of gravity.

7. I ALWAYS LIKED

I always liked Mickiewicz, though I didn't know why.

Then I realized that he was writing in cipher
And that this was a rule of poetry,
The distance between what we know and what we reveal.

In other words, it's what's inside the shell that matters.
And it's all right if readers play with shells.

The errors and childish conceptions of the explorers
Of mysteries should be forgiven.

I have been mocked because of Swedenborg and like nonsense,
For I transgressed the rules of literary fashion.

The louts grimaced sarcastically
As they discussed my pious, childish superstitions.

Which did not want to accept the only knowledge
Accessible to us: that people are created by people,
And that they, together, create something that they call truth.

While I wanted to believe in Adam and Eve, and in the Fall,
And in the hope of Restoration.

8. OH YES, I REMEMBER

Oh yes, I remember Romer's courtyard, where that lodge,
The Zealous Lithuanian, was located.

And in my old age I stood in the arcaded yard of my university, at the entrance of St. John's Church.

What a distance from here! And yet I was able to hear a driver's whip clacking as the carriage, with all of our company from Tuhanowicze, arrived at the front steps of the Chreptowicz's manor in Szczorsy.

To read in the largest library in Lithuania books adorned with a picture of Cosmic Man.

If, writing about me, they would mix up centuries, I could confirm that, yes, I was there in 1820, leaning over *L'Aurore naissante,* of Jakob Boehme, the French edition of 1802.

9. NOT OUT OF FRIVOLITY

Not out of frivolity, most reverend theologians, I busied myself with the secret knowledge of many centuries, but out of the pain in my heart when I looked out at the atrocity of the world.

If God is all-powerful, he can allow all this only if he is not good.

Wherefrom then the limits of his power? Why such an order of creation? They all tried to find an answer, heretics, kabbalists, alchemists, the Knights of the Rose Cross.

It's only today that they would find their intuitions confirmed in the assertions of astrophysicists that space and time are not at all eternal, that they had once their beginning.

In one unimaginable flash, which set ticking the clock of minutes, hours, centuries.

For that was what interested them precisely, what had happened in the bosom of the Deity before the flash, how Yes and No, good and evil came to be.

Jakob Boehme believed that the visible world arose as the effect of a catastrophe, as an act of God's mercy, to prevent the further spread of pure evil.

We complain that the earth is hell's antechamber: it might have been hell complete, without beauty, without goodness, not a ray.

10. WE HAVE READ IN THE CATECHISM

We have read in the catechism about a rebellion of angels—which presumes some activity in the pre-world, before the visible cosmos was created, for this is the only way we can think, in terms of "before" and "after."

Even if in the pre-world hosts of invisible angels existed, only one of them, manifesting his free will, rebelled, became the hetman of rebellion.

We don't know for certain whether he was the first and most perfect of beings called to existence, or simply the dark side of the very Deity, to whom Jakob Boehme gave the name "God's wrath-fire."

Be that as it may, an angel of great beauty and strength turned against the incomprehensible Unity, for he uttered the word "I," which meant separation.

Lucifer, bearer of dark light, also called Adversary, also called Satan; in the Book of Job the prosecutor in the service of the Creator.

There is no graver flaw in this oeuvre of the hands of the God who said "Yes" than this "No," this death, a shadow cast by the will toward separate existence.

That rebellion is a manifestation of one's proper "I" and is called desire, *concupiscentia,* and was repeated by our first parents. The tree of the knowledge of good and evil, as it was discovered by Adam and Eve, could also be called the tree of death.

And the sin of the world could be obliterated only by a new Adam, whose war against the Prince of This World is a war against death.

11. ACCORDING TO MICKIEWICZ

According to Mickiewicz and Jakob Boehme, Adam was like Adam Kadmon of the Kabbalah, the Cosmic Man in the bosom of Deity.

He appeared in created Nature, but he was angelic, endowed with an invisible body.

He was tempted by the forces of Nature, which addressed him thusly (as Mickiewicz dictated to Armand Lévy): "Here we are, evidences, shapes, things, demanding only to submit to you, to serve you. You see us. You touch us. You can direct us with a glance, a nod of the head. Have you seen a being higher than yourself? A God endowed with a glance and a nod who would give orders to the elements? Believe us, you are the true god, you are the master of creation. Marry us, let us become the same flesh, same nature, let us join to each other."

Adam succumbed to temptation and God sent him into deep sleep.

When he awoke, he saw Eve standing before him.

12. AND SO EVE

And so Eve proved to be the delegate of Nature and drew Adam down into a monotonous wheel of births and deaths.

As if she were the great Earth Mother of the Paleolith, giving birth, preserving ashes.

Thence perhaps man's fear before the promise of love, which is no different from the promise of death.

This earthliness of Eve, which will not find approval with our sisters, inclined Jakob Boehme to adopt the hypothesis of a New Eve, immaculate, who received and assented to an appeal to become the Mother of God.

Let us not forget that Boehme was speaking of a world of archetypes, a zone without before or after: in other words, Eve the second is not a successor to Eve the first; they stand side by side in the sight of God.

Changing one into the other, more closely related than sisters.

An astonishing "Hymn for the Annunciation of the Holy Lady Mary" was written by the young anticlerical Mickiewicz a short time before his Freemasonic hymn known as "Ode to Youth." He glorified Mary in the words of the prophet, i.e., Jakob Boehme.

13. IT'S NO WONDER

It's no wonder that such speculations arose,
for Original Sin is incomprehensible,
and becomes only a little clearer if we assume
that Adam was flattered to become
the master of all visible creation, and that Creation,
asking him to unite with it,
did so in the hope that he would save it from death.

That didn't happen, and he himself lost his immortality.

So it looks as if Original Sin
is just a Promethean dream about man,
a being so gifted that by the very force of his mind
he would create civilization and invent a cure for death.

And that a New Adam, Christ, assumed a body and died
in order to liberate us from Promethean pride.

Which pride, it is true, was a great difficulty for Mickiewicz.

14. YOU WHO WERE BORN

You who were born this night
To tear us from the Devil's might

— TRADITIONAL POLISH CAROL

Whoever considers as normal the order of things in which the strong
triumph, and the weak fail, and life ends with death, accepts the
devil's rule.

So Christianity should not pretend it looks favorably upon this world, for it sees at the core of it the sin of desire, or Universal Will, to use the term introduced by the great philosopher of pessimism, Schopenhauer, who found in Christianity and Buddhism a common trait: compassion for the inhabitants of earth, this vale of tears.

Whoever places his trust in Jesus Christ waits for His coming and the end of this world, when the first heaven and the first earth pass, and death is no more.

15. RELIGION COMES

Religion comes from our pity for humans.

They are too weak to live without divine protection.

Too weak to listen to the screeching noise of the turning of infernal wheels.

Who among us would accept a universe in which there was not one voice

Of compassion, pity, understanding?

To be human is to be completely alien amid the galaxies.

Which is sufficient reason for erecting, together with others, the temples of an unimaginable mercy.

16. TO TELL THE TRUTH

To tell the truth, I don't understand anything. There is only our ecstatic dance, a diminutive part of a great totality.

They are born and die; the dance doesn't stop. I cover my eyes, as if to protect them from the images rushing toward me.

Perhaps I only appropriate the gestures, words, and actions, proper to the small patch of time assigned to me.

Homo ritualis. Aware of it, I do what is prescribed for a one day's master.

17. WHY NOT CONCEDE

Why not concede that I have not progressed, in my religion, past the Book of Job?

With the one difference that Job thought of himself as innocent and I saw guilt in my genes.

I was not innocent; I wanted to be innocent, but I couldn't be.

I bore the misfortunes imposed on me without cursing God, as I have learned not to curse God for creating me as this, and not some other, man.

Misfortune was, according to me, the penalty for existing.

Day and night I addressed to God my question: Why? Uncertain to the end whether I understood His unclear answer.

18. HAD I NOT POSSESSED

Had I not possessed a certain familiarity with what is called pride, conceit, vanity,

I might have taken a little more seriously that spectacle that ends not so much with a curtain going down as with a thunderbolt from a cloudless sky.

But the comic force of the spectacle is so incomprehensible
that death seems an improper penalty for their self-regard,
their games and their treacherous successes.

I think of all this with sadness;
I know very well that I was a participant in these revels.

And then, I concede, it is difficult to believe in the immortal soul.

19. OH YES, YOU MUST DIE

Oh yes, you must die.
Death is immense, incomprehensible.
All Souls' Day: we want, in vain, to hear voices
From the dark, underground countries, Sheol, Hades.
We are rabbits, playing, unaware of the butcher's knife.
When the heart stops, my contemporaries say,
Shrugging their shoulders, that's it.

Christians lost their faith in the severe Judge
Who sentences sinners to kettles of boiling tar.

I profited from my reading of Swedenborg.

In whom no verdict falls from above,

And the souls of the dead are drawn, magnet-like, to similar souls.

By their karma, as the Buddhists say.

I feel in myself so much veiled evil
That I do not exclude myself from the possibility of hell.

It would probably be the hell of artists.

I.e., people who valued the perfection of their oeuvre

Over their duties as husbands, fathers, brothers, citizens.

20. A BORDER

I had a dream about a border, very difficult to cross, though I myself
had crossed a number of such borders despite the guardians of states
and empires.

In the dream everything was fine as long as we were not forced
to cross the border.

On this side a nappy green carpet made from the treetops of a tropical
forest, we soar over it, we birds.

On the other side nothing. Nothing to be touched, seen, heard, tasted.

We prepare to go there reluctantly, like émigrés who do not expect happiness in the distant countries of their exile.

21. AT LAST TO PRESENT

To present myself at last as an heir to mystical lodges, also as a man different from that of the legend.

Presumably a child of good fortune, who succeeds in everything, I gathered honors from a long, hardworking life.

Really, it happened quite differently from the way it appeared, yet out of pride and shame I abstained from confessions.

In my school years, the brutality of the football field persuaded me that I was unfit for struggle, and I began early to devise an alternative vocation.

Later I experienced real, not imaginary, tragedies, the more difficult to bear because I didn't consider myself entirely innocent.

I learned to bear misfortune the way one bears lameness, though my readers could hardly have guessed it from my writing.

Only a dark tone, an inclination toward a peculiar Manichean strain of Christianity, could have led one to the proper trail.

And, we should add, an entanglement of that individual in the history of the twentieth century, the absurdity of some of his actions, his narrow, miraculous escapes.

As if a substitute vocation had been confirmed, and the Good Lord had asked from me the completion of my oeuvre,

I toiled, I looked for greatness, the failure of which, I thought, could be attributed to the meanness of the era.

Finding greatness in others, sometimes in myself,
I was grateful for the gift of participation
in an extraordinary divine plan for mortals.

22. TREAT WITH UNDERSTANDING

Treat with understanding persons of weak faith.

Myself included. One day I believe, another I disbelieve.

Yet I feel warmth among people at prayer.
Since they believe, they help me to believe
in their existence, these incomprehensible beings.

I remember that they were made to be not much inferior to angels.

Under their ugliness, which is the stigma of their practical preoccupations, they are pure, and when they sing, a vein of ecstasy pulsates in their throats.

Most intensely before a statue of Holy Mary,
as she appeared to the young girl in Lourdes.

Naturally, I am a skeptic. Yet I sing with them,
thus overcoming the contradiction
between my private religion and the religion of the rite.

23. BEAUTIFUL LADY

Beautiful lady, You who appeared to the children at Lourdes and Fatima,

What astonished these children was Your loveliness, unsayable.

As if you wished to remind them that beauty is one of the components of the world.

Which I am able to confirm; I too have been a pilgrim in Lourdes by the grotto, where you hear the rustle of the river and see, in the pure blue sky above the mountains a narrow scrap of moon.

According to the testimonies, You stood above a little tree,
your feet about ten centimeters above the topmost leaves.

You had the body not of an apparition, but of some immaterial matter so that one could see the buttons of your dress.

Lady, I asked you for a miracle, though I was acutely aware

That I come from a country where Your sanctuaries
serve to strengthen a national illusion and provide the refuge
of Your—a pagan goddess's—protection against the invasion
of enemies.

My presence in such a place was disturbed

By my duty as a poet who should not flatter popular imaginings.

Yet who desires to remain faithful to Your unfathomable intention

When you appeared to the children at Fatima and Lourdes.

PART IV

APPRENTICE

I.

Among the lawns at Marienbad
A young man takes a walk.
Lean, slightly stooped, dark-haired.
He swings his cane, though he is visibly sad.
He does not like *la Belle Epoque,*
He hardly tolerates his poet friends
From Closerie des Lilas and the Kalissaya bar.
He would have liked to have been born earlier, like Lord Byron,
Whose many stanzas he knows by heart.

"Apprentice": The hero of this poem is a man to whom I attach the title of master. Thus a title befitting me is that of apprentice. So only the relation between two persons is involved here, not an apprenticeship in a guild or some other institution.

Marienbad: Before the first World War, international society flocked to this Bohemian town for its famous "waters." After her estate in Czereia had been sold in 1906, the mother of Oscar Milosz moved from there to Warsaw. She and her son, then living in Paris, would meet in Marienbad occasionally, including in 1911.

Closerie des Lilas and the Kalissaya bar: These were Parisian cafés frequented by poets of the late Symbolist era. Jean Moreas and the aging Oscar Wilde were among the customers at Kalissaya, "the first American bar in Paris." O. Milosz often turned up in an English-speaking milieu, where he befriended Christian Gauss and Nathalie Clifford Barney. Barney, still famous today for her defiantly lesbian style, conducted a rather snobbish literary salon, into which she introduced O. Milosz in 1913. She also became his close platonic friend and confidante.

Or at least in the time of his grandparents,
The heroic Arthur and the pretty Natalia Tassistro,
Daughter of an old Genoan family.
Not for him such a father as he'd been given:
An athletic, violent Don Juan.
Or the too-possessive love of his mother, Miriam Rosenthal.
In Czereia he would hide in the thickets of the half-abandoned park.

The biography of this man is, in my opinion, as important
As the lives of saints and prophets are,
For it goes well beyond merely literary interest.
He himself, it is true, didn't for a long time know his vocation.

His grandparents: He describes them in papers which can be found in the archive of the Lithuanian legation in Paris. Arthur: "Officer, at the age of nineteen in a regiment of uhlans in the Polish-Lithuanian Army, took part in the campaign of 1831 against the Russians. At the Battle of Ostroleka he lost his left leg, torn off by a cannonball. He married an Italian cantatrice, very graceful and talented, daughter of the conductor of La Scala in Milan, from an ancient but impoverished Genoan family. I possess letters of my grandfather which testify to his good heart and good education. He considered his wife a model of charm and all virtues. My grandmother and grandfather made an exceptionally beautiful and noble couple. All the feelings that I would normally have directed toward my father and mother I felt, because of strange coincidences and psychological complications, toward my grandparents, and my love for them found its reflection in my person. Looks apart, I am a kind of physical and moral amalgam of Arthur Milosz and Natalia Tassistro."

Not for him such a father: Wladyslaw Milosz, son of Arthur and Natalia, was born in Wilno in 1838. He became a legend in the society chronicles of the nineteenth century because of his exotic outlook, his strength, his adventurous lifestyle, and his amorous conquests. He brought to Czereia a Jewish beauty whom he had met by chance. Miriam Rosenthal was born in Staniszow in 1858. Thus, she was younger by twenty years than her seducer. According to the testimony of the son: "I was never able to give expression to my tenderness toward my parents. My father was a violent and a sick man. My mother, with a solicitude entirely material and uncomprehending, annoyed me so much that I very early got into the habit of hiding myself in the most inaccessible spots in the park and gardens to get rid of the emotions provoked by her presence." Let us note that the simultaneous baptism and first communion of the son, who was born in 1877, took place in 1886 at St. Alexander's Church in Warsaw.

I have read books about him, and the testimony
        of his contemporaries,
Visiting in my imagination the terrain
Of the declining decades of the Czarist Empire.
Country of the black grouse, the moose and the bear.
The masters drink, hunt, play cards.
And nearby Byelorussian peasants with their sunken faces,
With their fleeting, hostile looks,
And Jews, debilitated by misery,
Their women with the eyes of witches,
Contorted, wrapped in shawls,
Devastated from giving birth like animals.

Miriam's son suffered as few human hearts suffer.
"Cold and insanity wandered aimlessly through the house."
He always remembered his nurse with gratitude,
Good Marie Weld from Alsace,
Driven by her need for employment to those wild regions.
As for his tutor, Mr. Doboszynski, he is responsible
For the longish poems of his protégé
About the battle at Kircholmem and King Sobieski.

Country of the black grouse: The estate of Czereia embraced forests practically untouched by the axe. *A Guide through Lithuania and Byelorussia,* by Napoleon Rouba, published in Wilno in 1909, gives the following information: "Czereia, town and estate situated in the district of Senno, *gubernia* of Mohylev, by lake, thirty-eight versts from Senno. Once the huge holding of the Sapiehas family, population above three thousand. The town is quite commercial, the nearest railway station, Krupka on the Moscow-Brzesc line, is thirty-five versts distant. Main products for export: lumber and woodcraft. The parish church is of stone, with a miraculous painting of St. Michael the

Apostle. A district office, a school, a pharmacy, a fiscal office. At present the main area of the estate, about 6,000 desatins in size, is the property of the Milosz family. The soil is clayish, fertile." The description of the inhabitants in my text is a paraphrase of Oscar Milosz. The passage is quoted in my book *Searching for a Homeland.*

The longish poems: The protégé had in his childhood already learned French and German, and was to become a poet who wrote in French. He did not, however, abandon Polish, as is proved by his excellent translation into French of the ballad "Lilies" by Mickiewicz and by a volume of poems in Polish presented to a Warsaw publisher in 1904, the manuscript of which has been lost.

It was perhaps an act of cruelty
To leave him alone in Paris in a lycée.
He grew up to be a French poet with the stigma of a dilettante,
For he had also inherited a fabulous fortune
In mast-sized pine trees. And that is a bad combination.

On the first of January in the year 1901,
For the very opening of the twentieth century,
Nonchalantly, with a cigarette hanging from his lips,
He shot himself in the heart, and the doctors gave him no hope.
I would have remained without my admired teacher.
We would have remained, as we were already, a small religious
    order,
Seekers of the Sun of Memory,
Readers of his treatise *Ars Magna*.

It was perhaps an act of cruelty: In 1889 his parents took him to Paris and left him as an *interne,* a boarder, at the Lycée Janson de Sailly. Later he lived with the family of the well-known pedagogue, Professor Maurice Petit.

In mast-sized pine trees: The very tall and straight pine trees from the forests of that area were exported mostly to England, where they were used by ship-builders. Such was the wealth of the estate of Czereia. Before World War I Oscar Milosz had a reputation as a very rich dilettante who wrote poetry as a hobby. This led to unpleasant misunderstandings, for instance, when he refused to finance a theatrical initiative of André Gide, who swore vengeance and kept his oath by seeing to it that Milosz was, for several dozen years, blackballed by the Parisian publisher Gallimard.

On the first of January: This information is taken from a letter from Oscar Milosz to Christian Gauss dated February 12, 1901. Milosz was twenty-three.

Seekers of the Sun of Memory: The secret of being is contained in the very movement of the blood, yet man has lost knowledge of it. In his poem "Memoria," Milosz wrote: "Yet this is, my son, what humans, who created God and the universe, call instinct, or the instinct of self-preservation, and what we, uniquely situated in the Place, call the Sun of Memory."

His treatise Ars Magna: That book, whose title refers to a name given once to alchemy, was published in Paris in 1924. It was composed of five metaphysical poems: I. "The Letter to Storge," II. "Memoria," III. "Numbers," IV. "Turba Magna," and V. "Lumen." "The Letter to Storge" was written in 1916. *Storge* is a Greek word describing the kind of love that parents have for their children. With such care the author turns to future generations. I have translated *Ars Magna* and another treatise-poem, "Les Arcanes," from French into English for *The Noble Traveler,* a selection of Oscar Milosz's writings published by Lindisfarne Press in 1984. A translation of *Ars Magna* into Polish forms part of my volume *Storge,* published by Znak in 1993. "The Letter to Storge" presents a cosmological exposition that corresponds precisely to Einstein's theory of relativity, even though the author was then unaware of Einstein's discovery, which implied a rejection of eternal space and eternal time (i.e., of the cosmology of Isaac Newton).

II.

I often think of Venice, which returns like a musical motif,
From the time of my first visit there before the war,
When I saw on the beach at Lido
The goddess Diana in the form of a German girl,
To the last when, after burying Joseph Brodsky,
We feasted at the Palazzo Mocenigo, the very one
In which Lord Byron had lived.
And there were the chairs of the cafés in the Piazza San Marco.
That's where Oscar Milosz, solitary wanderer,
Came under sentence in 1909:
He beheld the love of his life, Emmy von Heine-Geldern,
Whom he called till the day of his death "my beloved wife,"
And who married Baron Leo Salvotti von Eichencraft
    und Bindenburg
And died in Vienna in the second half of the century.

When I saw on the beach at Lido: A beautiful German girl appears in my "Six Lectures in Verse" from 1987.

After burying Joseph Brodsky: The body of Joseph Brodsky, who died in New York City in 1996, was, in accordance with his wishes, transported to Venice and buried in the cemetery of San Michele on the twenty-first of June, 1997. Paradoxically, his tomb and the tomb of Ezra Pound are contiguous.

We feasted at the Palazzo Mocenigo: Byron stayed there for some time in 1818 and it was there, in the early months of 1819, that he began his *Don Juan.*

Emmy von Heine-Geldern: She was born in 1890 in Vienna, a younger daughter of Baron Gustav von Heine-Geldern and his wife, Regine, a relation of the poet Heinrich Heine. She died in Vienna in the 1960s. O. M. called Emmy his celestial wife. The marriage between them never occurred because of the intrigues of his mother, though we do not know the reasons for her opposition. When Emmy married another man in 1910, O. M. was thirty-three. It is difficult, therefore, to suspect him of bowing to his mother's will.

In that hymn to the glory of God and man
Which is *Miguel Mañara*
He introduces the character of Miguel's wife,
The youthful Girolama, because of whom
Juliusz Osterwa did not do the play at Reduta,
Because he searched in vain for an actress to carry the role.

I read *Miguel Mañara* in Bronislawa Ostrowska's translation
At the age of fourteen. It had to be so.
I was spellbound by the beauty of Girolama. Which did me no good,
Since it encouraged my search for a perfect love,
That romantic mirroring of souls
That proves to be a safe venture for very few people.

Miguel Mañara: This mystery play was written by O. M. at the end of 1911 and published in *La Nouvelle Revue Française* in 1912. The character of Don Miguel had his prototype in an historical Don Juan, Miguel Mañara Vincentelo de Leca, who was born in 1629 in Seville and died a repentant sinner and saintly monk. Pope John Paul II conferred on him in 1986 the title "Servant of God," which is the first step toward beatification.

Girolama: The Polish translator of *Miguel Mañara,* Bronislawa Ostrowska, and her husband, Stanislaw Ostrowski, belonged in 1912 to the Society of Polish Artists, which was located on rue Denfert-Rochereau in Paris. One of its founders was O. M. The outbreak of World War I made the publication of the translation impossible, and it did not appear until 1919, when it was included in a volume of Milosz's poems, *Poezje,* published by Zdroj in Poznan. Ostrowska's translation of *Miguel Mañara* belongs to the history of Polish theater. It had many admirers among theater directors, including Wilam Horzyca, Leon Schiller, Juliusz Osterwa, and Tadeusz Byrski, as well as Rhapsodic Theater group members Mieczyslaw Kotlarczyk and

Karol Wojtyla, later known as Pope John Paul II. Juliusz Osterwa, who undertook to produce the play, felt that the role of Girolama could only be played by an actress who was practically approaching sainthood herself, a circumstance which tended to delay any actual staging. Tadeusz Byrski, from Osterwa's theater ensemble Reduta, directed a radio production for Poland's Imaginary Theater in 1935. Osterwa directed public readings of the play in Warsaw in 1937 and 1938. The second production was broadcast on Polish State Radio. The unofficial Polish premiere was perhaps a staging by the students at the State Theatrical School in Warsaw in 1937. The official premiere occurred as late as 1991 at the Contemporary Theater in Szczecin, directed by Wieslaw Gorski. Ostrowska's translation was reissued, together with Irena Slawinska's versions of two other of O. M.'s mystery plays, *Mephiboseth* and *Paul de Tarse,* in the volume *Misteria,* published by Lublin's Catholic University Press in 1999.

I see, in this absolutizing of love,
The fruit of misogyny,
The habit of opposing an ideal woman to real ones.

So Venice sets sail like a great ship of death,
On its deck a swarming crowd of people changed into ghosts.
I said my farewell at San Michele by Joseph's grave and Ezra
    Pound's.
The city was ready, of course, to receive the crowds of the unborn
For whom we will be just an enigmatic legend.

III.

I came to believe that what he said was true.
I was a man inclined to adoration,
Convinced that one could recognize greatness
And should keep the secret.

I knew that he had committed the sin of despair.
Pitying him I deflected my pity for myself.
Yet it was he who received a sacra from above
And his pride was the pride of a king.

The Nobel prize is enough for the smaller ones.
It would not commend itself to someone who gave
    an incomprehensible gift
And announced the planetary victory of the Roman church.

We have been charged with preserving that gift
And protecting it from the noise of the mass media.

The Nobel prize: When a certain Polish writer received the Nobel prize in
1980, some French newspapers expressed the opinion that it had been given
to the wrong Milosz.

IV.

In one of his letters to Christian Gauss,
He describes his seasons in Czereia.
Horseback riding in the forest in summer, reading in winter.
Smoking his pipe under a lamp with a green glass shade,
He reread Schopenhauer, Kant, and Plato,
Traveled, as he said, with Don Quixote to Spain
And to Italy with Heine.

It was then that he added Russian to his Polish, French, German,
    and English,
Watched the revolution of 1905,
Which contributed to his later opinion about communism:
"Too bloody an enterprise for modest social progress."

In one of his letters to Christian Gauss: The description of his stay in Czereia
occurs in a letter to Christian Gauss written in January 1904.

Many years later I happened to spend a night at a model collective
   farm in Labunava,
Hiding a smile, for I remembered how he had mythologized
   our family
Which had come presumably from Labunowo vel Hanusewicz vel
   Serbiny.

I felt no connection, except perhaps a little to the cemetery
   at Wedziagola.

A model collective farm in Labunava: I spent a night there in 1992, since there
was no hotel in the neighboring town of Kedainai, during my first trip back
to Lithuania after a fifty-two-year absence.

Had mythologized our family: O. M. wrote (in the Lithuanian archives):
"Though a century and a half has elapsed since the separation of the two
branches of our family, the cordial relations between the Lithuanian
Miloszes and the Byelorussian Miloszes have never been weakened. From
early youth my father implanted in me the sense of attachment and respect
with which our Byelorussian branch of the family regarded the Lithuanian
Miloszes."

Labunowo vel Hanusewicz vel Serbiny: About Labunowo, in Lithuanian
Labunava, we read in the *Guide through Lithuania and Byelorussia* of
Napoleon Rouba the following: "Labunowo, a village and manor on the
Niewiaza River, at the confluence with the Berupia River, in Kowno *guber-
nia* and the Kowno district. A beautiful, picturesque countryside. The
wooden parish church was founded by the Zabiellos. The estate of around
4,000 desatins of very fertile soil is the property of Count Zabiello. A fine
brick palace with a park by the Niewiaza. There is a ferry across the river."
   Serbiny, which neighbors on Labunowo, was the ancestral estate of the

Miloszes. Hanusewicz was also, for a while, among their possessions. Whether they ever owned Labunowo is not known.

The cemetery at Wedziagola: A few kilometers from Labunowo and Serbiny, Wedziagola, Wandziogala in Lithuanian, was once upon a time a cluster of cottages of the petty gentry, who even attempted in 1918 to create an independent "Wedziagola Republic." Until relatively recent times some tombs of seventeenth- and eighteenth-century Miloszes survived there, as well as the grave of my grandfather Arthur Milosz, who perhaps was named to honor his cousin in the Byelorussian line.

v.

I was very young when I first felt depressed by the idea of eternally
    existing matter,

And of time stretching backward and forward forever.

It contradicted my image of God the Creator,
For what would he have to do in a universe everlasting?

So I read "The Letter to Storge" like a revelation,
Learning that time and space had a beginning,
That they appeared in a flash together with so-called matter,
Just as medieval scholars from Oxford to Chartres had guessed,
Through a *transmutatio* of divine light into light merely physical.

How much that changed my poems! They were dedicated
    to the contemplation of time
Behind which, since that moment, eternity transpired.
Though I was dissatisfied with my writing, which was provisional,
Namely, of that kind in which what is most important remains
    hidden.

Of course, I was guilty of folly and trespasses.
I pronounced the name of a woman and it seemed she was standing
    by.
And yet I could not make a confession of my life,
For good and evil were too deeply entangled in my egoistic oeuvre.

"The Letter to Storge": This poem puts forth the hypothesis that the universe
originated in an unimaginable flash that gave birth to space, time, and

matter. Many decades later the same hypothesis was advanced in the form of the Big Bang Theory.

As medieval scholars . . . had guessed: Scholars from Oxford and Chartres maintained that before the creation of the world there was nonphysical divine light. God's *Fiat lux* was a transmutation of this nonphysical light.

For good and evil were too deeply entangled: The creation of works of art is marked by an astonishing duality: on the one hand it is a completely disinterested activity, even altruistic, consisting of detaching oneself from oneself; on the other hand it consists in feeding one's egoistic ambition. Whenever creative work enters personal life and makes its demand there, honest self-examination is very difficult. An oeuvre does not exonerate. And yet it is not quite "egoistic," though it introduces into a life many complications.

VI.

Through many afternoons in the library at the Sorbonne,
I pored over a doctoral dissertation
On the mysticism of Milosz.
Its author, an American named Stanley Guise,
After he renounced his scholarly career in Paris,
Returned to America and became a gardener.

His treatise reproduces faithfully many notes
That Oscar scrawled in the margins of an English edition
      of Swedenborg.
The notes are in French, English,
And, in more emotional moods, Polish.

For instance when he found what seemed a description of his own
      initiation,
He exclaimed, "In the name of the Father, the Son, and the Holy
Spirit. Amen. The night between the 14th and 15th December 1914."

He also comments in Polish on the spiritual sun in Swedenborg:
"My sun moved from my brow up to the summit of my cranium,
So it was probably the angel of Jehovah."

An English edition of Swedenborg: The majority of the notes were made in the
margins of *Vera Christiana religio,* which book is divided into numbered
paragraphs. Some notes come from the margins of another book, *Conjugal
Love.* Though he treated Swedenborg as a celestial guide, he treats his de-
scriptions of Heaven and Hell somewhat critically, seeing in them an attempt
to get out of the spaces that our minds so incessantly multiply and divide. He
also remarks: "I dislike it when someone talks as if he had breakfast every

week with God." Yet he conceded that Swedenborg had a gift for seeing things he himself had also experienced.

The night between the 14th and 15th December 1914: The mystical experience referred to in "The Letter to Storge."

He called Goethe his spiritual guide,
Swedenborg his celestial guide,
Though he treated his descriptions of Heaven and Hell with humor:
"My God," he wrote (in French), "send me wherever you like,
But not to the paradise of the English,
(Or the hell of the Russians).
Make me a shoe-shine boy for Prussian angels,
Anything but the English paradise,
Anything but the English paradise!"

Unexpectedly, but precisely like Swedenborg,
Who reproached Roman Catholics for having three Gods,
He found, like William Blake before him,
A confirmation of human nature in the Old Testament God
Who had chosen the planet Earth from among the innumerable
          worlds.

"Christ is Jehovah, incarnate,
Made accessible to man: only through the Son
Do we approach the Father; the Son and the Holy Ghost
Are but attributes of the Father—
This is the whole doctrine of Swedenborg."

He had read no mystics before that December night in 1914.

A confirmation of human nature: Swedenborg criticized the doctrine of the
Holy Trinity because it was completely incomprehensible and in effect a doc-
trine of three gods. Instead, he wrote, "Christ is Jehovah accessible to man."
The difference between this construction and that of the Catholic Church is
the object of a long theological dispute.

It was probably from Swedenborg that he took his symbolism
  of Adam and Eve
And his version of the Fall in which all of First Nature
Was changed into Second Nature, grieving.

An idea not altogether clear to me, for Swedenborg
Speaks of a civilization of preadamites and adamites,
So one must ask whether for these people
The lion did in fact lie down with the lamb.

Human beings should approach, trembling and with reverence,
That deepest arcanum, the union of a man and a woman.
It is an unveiling of the incomprehensible
Love of the Creator for creation.
And the loss of that memory by the twentieth century was unlucky.
They changed the Song of Songs into a sexual game.

Milosz rejected the physicalizing of spiritual space in Swedenborg,
With its heaven and hell parallel to our earthly space,
But he venerates his master as a messenger
Who brought important tidings to a Christian.

His symbolism of Adam and Eve: Swedenborg divided the time of civilization
over the millennia into a sequence of several "churches," i.e., civilizations
succeeding each other. Adam, in his writings, symbolizes a primitive civi-
lization of "adamites."

The Fall in which all of First Nature: O. M. believed profoundly (and in ac-
cordance with the Catholic catechism) that in Paradise Nature was perfect
and did not know death. The Fall (*prevarication*) of Adam not only changed
the situation of man, making him mortal, but also introduced death and suf-

fering into the whole of nature. Since that moment a pained Second Nature grieves and yearns to return to its lost happiness, which can be accomplished again only through man. Nota bene: Here we see the radical anthropocentrism of biblical religion.

The deepest Arcanum: The sexual union of man and woman occupies a central place in Swedenborg's system, which is, on the whole, highly erotic. O. M. had a similar outlook. See, particularly, the chapter "Memoria" in *Ars Magna.* In the Bible the most important book in this respect is the Song of Songs, in which carnal love is at the same time a metaphor for the Creator's love of creation.

The physicalizing of spiritual space: In other words, the descriptions of the beyond in Swedenborg were for him like the descriptions of hell, purgatory, and paradise in Dante. They came from a basic human need to "situate," to assign to all our images a location in space.

VII.

Diplomatic notes written in a polished French,
Speeches before the League of Nations,
A treatise on the future United States of Europe,
Warnings about a war approaching on the Roan Horse
Of the Apocalypse, a war which would begin in Gdansk
    and Gdynia.
All that he did, this symbolist poet, as duty to mankind
Was an act of contrition for his individualist's daydreams.
He chose Lithuania, a small country of solid and hardworking
    peasants.
With tenderness he leaned in his thoughts over each man, woman,
    and child.

And so it should be, that we spend our lives in the everyday bustle,
Trying to be in agreement with the line of our fate.

Diplomatic notes: Having committed himself to the independence of Lithuania, O. M. was a providential figure for the Lithuanian delegation to the peace conference at Versailles. The French were surprised by the sophistication of the diplomatic notes coming from the Lithuanian delegation and it got their notice. For O.M. his endeavors on behalf of Lithuania fulfilled his desire to serve humanity; this desire can be guessed from the poems written after the mystical night in 1914 (e.g., "Nihumim"). He became the first Lithuanian ambassador to Paris and was active in the League of Nations. (His adversary there, in the debate over the future of the city of Wilno, was the famous Polish historian Szymon Aszkenazy, who came from an illustrious Jewish family. He maintained that the city should belong to Poland. O. M. claimed it for Lithuania. They quarreled in Polish.) Thus he fulfilled his life not only through words, but in his actions. In his political writings he advanced the idea of a United States of Europe and warned against Germany, which, he said, was no more than superficially democratic. Ten years before the events of 1939, he foresaw the outbreak of war in the corridor separating Poland from East Prussia.

VIII.

Religion ceased to be in my mind a national rite.

What remained was to meditate on two millennia of Christianity,
    its peoples and lands.

Its doctrines, the crimes and follies committed in its name.

But also on the activity of a succession of valiant personalities,

Of saints, and heretics later made equal to saints.

I would not dare to assign to myself a priestly function.

I was no more than an apprentice to a master of alchemy.

In Florence, for instance, around the year 1500

When humanists were reading the Zohar and other books
    of the Kabbalah.

Religion ceased to be in my mind a national rite: My religious crisis in high school deprived me of the secure faith of a Polish Catholic and set me searching. In that search the guidance of Oscar Milosz was considerable, though not exclusive.

I was no more than an apprentice: I consider him the successor to alchemists and Rosicrucians, just as he presented himself in his writings. This was not without connection to my need for mystery. And he, after all, considered mystery an important ingredient in poetry.

In Florence, for instance: Around this date we can locate the beginning of those theological and theosophical speculations that paralleled the progress of Renaissance science. Neoplatonists of that time were avid readers of the Kabbalah, finding there many similarities to their own intuitions. The expulsion of the Jews from Spain in 1492 facilitated European contact with Judaism, which enriched in the sixteenth and seventeenth centuries the thought of Jakob Boehme and Paracelsus.

Or in Lyon, when ladies listened to Mozart at a lodge that went back
    to the Templars.

Places and times were simultaneous for me,

Fused in the labyrinth of the movement of the stars.

I touched fans, I heard the rustling of skirts,

I used to put on masks, change costumes.

The whole arrangement of the world seemed ominous to my heart.

Like the Albigensians, I yearned for liberation.

But *storge,* a tutelary love, instructed me,

And I learned to be grateful.

Or in Lyon: The eighteenth century knew "mystical lodges," i.e., groups of freemasons not satisfied with rationalism and inclined to look for an esoteric interpretation of Christianity. The principle figures in these lodges were Martínez Pasqualis and Louis-Claude de Saint-Martin, both of whom strongly influenced Adam Mickiewicz. The Masonic lodges of the eighteenth century liked to consider themselves as continuators and avengers of the Knights Templar.

Like the Albigensians: The Albigensians, or the Cathari, considered the world of matter utterly evil—in this they are successors to the Manicheans—and they permitted suicide by refusing food, the so-called *endura,* or holy famine.

IX.

For a long time I tried to find out the task prepared for me.
Provided it was not too difficult for my modest strengths.

I observed the tone and style of my time

In order to act against it in the poetry of my native language,

Which meant not allowing it to lose a sense of hierarchy

And by hierarchy meant what a child means:

One obeisance, rather than a series of idols which appear
        and disappear.

The sublime doesn't have fame or money on its side.

But it persists, it renews itself in every generation.

Because in thought some greatness of soul keeps being born.

So it is important to know how to repeat after Goethe:

Respect! Respect! Respect!

PART V

ORPHEUS AND EURYDICE

Standing on flagstones of the sidewalk at the entrance to Hades
Orpheus hunched in a gust of wind
That tore at his coat, rolled past in waves of fog,
Tossed the leaves of the trees. The headlights of cars
Flared and dimmed in each succeeding wave.

He stopped at the glass-paneled door, uncertain
Whether he was strong enough for that ultimate trial.

He remembered her words: "You are a good man."
He did not quite believe it. Lyric poets
Usually have—as he knew—cold hearts.
It is like a medical condition. Perfection in art
Is given in exchange for such an affliction.

Only her love warmed him, humanized him.
When he was with her, he thought differently about himself.
He could not fail her now, when she was dead.

He pushed open the door and found himself walking in a labyrinth,
Corridors, elevators. The livid light was not light but the dark
    of the earth.
Electronic dogs passed him noiselessly.
He descended many floors, a hundred, three hundred, down.

He was cold, aware that he was Nowhere.
Under thousands of frozen centuries,
On an ashy trace where generations had moldered,
In a kingdom that seemed to have no bottom and no end.

Thronging shadows surrounded him.
He recognized some of the faces.
He felt the rhythm of his blood.

He felt strongly his life with its guilt
And he was afraid to meet those to whom he had done harm.
But they had lost the ability to remember
And gave him only a glance, indifferent to all that.

For his defense he had a nine-stringed lyre.
He carried in it the music of the earth, against the abyss
That buries all of sound in silence.
He submitted to the music, yielded
To the dictation of a song, listening with rapt attention,
Became, like his lyre, its instrument.

Thus he arrived at the palace of the rulers of that land.
Persephone, in her garden of withered pear and apple trees,
Black, with naked branches and verrucose twigs,
Listened from the funereal amethyst of her throne.

He sang the brightness of mornings and green rivers,
He sang of smoking water in the rose-colored daybreaks,
Of colors: cinnabar, carmine, burnt sienna, blue,
Of the delight of swimming in the sea under marble cliffs,
Of feasting on a terrace above the tumult of a fishing port,
Of the tastes of wine, olive oil, almonds, mustard, salt.
Of the flight of the swallow, the falcon,
Of a dignified flock of pelicans above a bay,
Of the scent of an armful of lilacs in summer rain,
Of his having composed his words always against death
And of having made no rhyme in praise of nothingness.

I don't know—said the goddess—whether you loved her or not.
Yet you have come here to rescue her.
She will be returned to you. But there are conditions:
You are not permitted to speak to her, or on the journey back

To turn your head, even once, to assure yourself that she is
    behind you.

And so Hermes brought forth Eurydice.
Her face no longer hers, utterly gray,
Her eyelids lowered beneath the shade of her lashes.
She stepped rigidly, directed by the hand
Of her guide. Orpheus wanted so much
To call her name, to wake her from that sleep.
But he refrained, for he had accepted the conditions.

And so they set out. He first, and then, not right away,
The slap of the god's sandals and the light patter
Of her feet fettered by her robe, as if by a shroud.
A steep climbing path phosphorized
Out of darkness like the walls of a tunnel.
He would stop and listen. But then
They stopped, too, and the echo faded.
And when he began to walk the double tapping commenced again.
Sometimes it seemed closer, sometimes more distant.
Under his faith a doubt sprang up
And entwined him like cold bindweed.
Unable to weep, he wept at the loss
Of the human hope for the resurrection of the dead,
Because he was, now, like every other mortal.
His lyre was silent, yet he dreamed, defenseless.
He knew he must have faith and he could not have faith.
And so he would persist for a very long time,
Counting his steps in a half-wakeful torpor.

Day was breaking. Shapes of rock loomed up
Under the luminous eye of the exit from underground.

It happened as he expected. He turned his head
And behind him on the path was no one.

Sun. And sky. And in the sky white clouds.
Only now everything cried to him: Eurydice!
How will I live without you, my consoling one!
But there was a fragrant scent of herbs, the low humming of bees,
And he fell asleep with his cheek on the sun-warmed earth.